Grand-o-grams

postcards to keep in touch with your grandkids all-year-round

by Marianne Richmond

Grand-o-grams

Any season is a reason to be in touch with
your grandchildren! Use these 40 fun
postcards to say hello, send a hug, or to
remind them how much you love them.
You may even inspire a return letter!

Dear Bobby,
It sure was fun to see
you on your summer
vacation! Thanks for
collecting the shells
on the beach for me.
Have a great year at
school. See you soon!
Love, Grandma

Bobby Smith
425 Maple Street

Grand-o-grams

This postcard book is part of The Gifts of being Grand
product collection, inspired by the well-loved gift book,
The Gifts of being Grand, a tribute to the special
joys and rewards of grandparenthood,
written and illustrated by Marianne Richmond.

Marianne Richmond Studios, Inc.
420 N. 5th Street, Suite 840
Minneapolis, MN 55401
www.mariannerichmond.com

ISBN 0-9753528-7-3

Text and illustrations by Marianne Richmond

Book design by Sara Dare Biscan and Meg Anderson

Printed in China

Second Printing

To a cool grandson

To a sweet granddaughter

Hey Sunshine!

Hope to "sea" you soon!

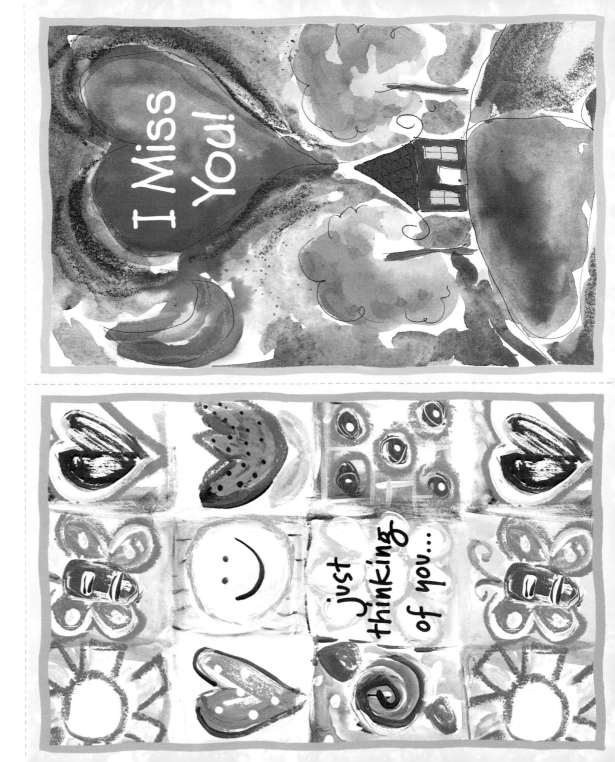

I'm blue without you...

Write Back!

Hope you're having a good day!
Juggling 101
Adventure Travel
YOU CAN SUCCEED!
How to Grow

miss you

Thinking
of you

i miss you...

Happy Valentine's Day

to a wonderful grandchild!

Happy Valentine's Day

Happy Easter!

Happy Easter!

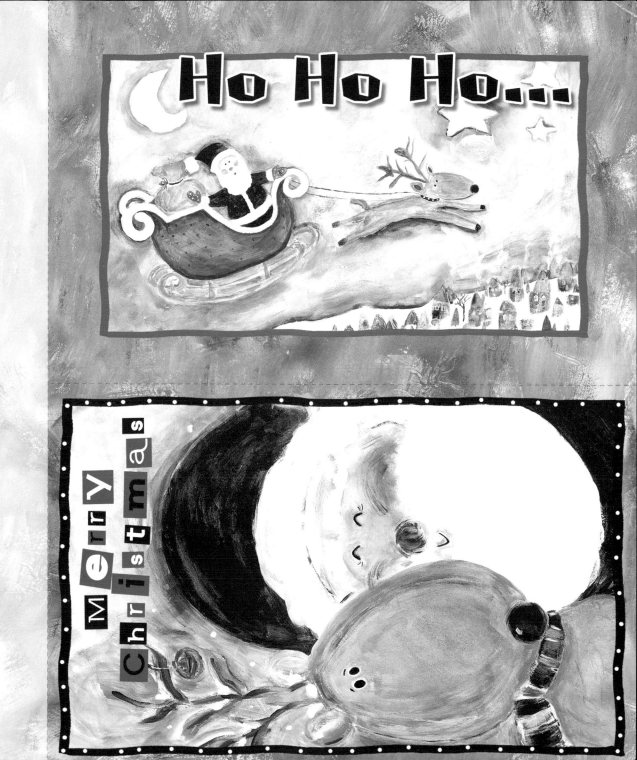